THE YELLOW ROOM

poems by

Amy Gordon

Finishing Line Press
Georgetown, Kentucky

THE YELLOW ROOM

Copyright © 2022 by Amy Gordon
ISBN 978-1-64662-974-9 First Edition
All rights reserved under International and Pan-American Copyright Conventions. No part of this book may be reproduced in any manner whatsoever without written permission from the publisher, except in the case of brief quotations embodied in critical articles and reviews.

ACKNOWLEDGMENTS

Grateful acknowledgement to these journals or contest pamphlets where a version of these poems first appeared:

Blue Nib: Radiant Geranium;
Palette Poetry: A Call for 19th Century Poets
Poets' Seat Contest: On Learning There Are no Further Treatment Options for My Husband
Straw Dog Writers' Guild Pandemic Poetry: The Verb to Be
*Tiny Seed Journa*l: Plain Song
Wheeler Memorial Library Contest: Bequest; How They Once Leapt

With heartfelt thanks to the Wednesday/Friday poets and the Gatehouse poets.

Publisher: Leah Huete de Maines
Editor: Christen Kincaid
Cover Art and Design: Jane Low-Beer; Richard Peachey
Author Photo: Timothy C. Young

Order online: www.finishinglinepress.com
also available on amazon.com

Author inquiries and mail orders:
Finishing Line Press
PO Box 1626
Georgetown, Kentucky 40324
USA

Table of Contents

On Learning There Are No Further Treatment Options for My Husband 1
How Brave He Is 3
How Should You Read the Moon? 4
After the Tsunami 5
Bargaining 6
Fear 7
Sing to the Boys 8
A Call for 19th Century Painters 9
How They Once Leapt 10
Creating Trails 11
The Verb To Be 12
Adjusting 13
A New Country 14
Bequest 15
Monster 16
On the Flight from Boston to San Francisco 17
Ennui 18
The Hike 19
Phantom Dog 20
Plain Song 21
Cricket Song 22
My Invention 23
Flight 24
Radiant Geraniums 27
The Fig Tree 28

For Hugh and Bridget

On Learning There Are No Further Treatment Options for My Husband

Stare into the yellow room.
Stand at the edge of the threshold.
Look for clues.

On the table: a pair of embroidery scissors
forged to look like a stork.
Lovely item! So pretty!

Object as metaphor. Must examine.
Stork brings new life. And scissors?
Instrument of the Fates?

A snuff box beside the scissors.
People used to stuff powdered
tobacco up their noses

to makes them sneeze.
O People, how strange thou art.
A candle can be snuffed out,

or a life. Cut Delete Start over
Enter the yellow room.
Yellow, meaning butterfly, golden-rod, butter.

Sometimes words are just sounds.
Stork Snuff Cut Yellow
Say yellow. Yellow

meaning a blouse hanging inside
a dark closet, a lantern held in the hand.
I need yellow. I need mornings

crayoned with a child's yellow sun.
I need to undress from the night.
To wear a yellow blouse.

Is lightning yellow?
I had a teacher once who wrote
lightning and *lightening* on the board.

Don't confuse these, she said. She stood
with chalk, like Zeus ready to strike us dead.
Then came the test. Even as I wrote the words

I was afraid— more afraid of her
than of walking in an open field
during a thunderstorm.

Here the yellow and blue
carpet's patterned with white
chrysanthemums—in some cultures

the flower of weddings; in others,
of mourning. *Chrysos* means golden
and *Mum* is the name I called

when I needed my mother.
Mum's the word. Shh, listen.
The window's wide open.

He is mowing the lawn.
Trees cast black lace on the grass.
I look through a pair of binoculars.

Light curves the lens of glass
through which I spy.
How small he has grown.

Am I looking through the wrong end?
I sit down in the yellow room.
I write *lightning*.

How Brave He Is

When he dreams in the still night,
he steals back whole minutes, the ones
he lost in the cancer chair.

Buttons on his pajamas slip sideways,
freed from certainty. He dreams wild,
sails deep into salty seas. Stars

startle when his eyes open.
The Big Dipper dips close, scoops
mortal pain into its deep bowl.

By sunrise he has forgotten
what the day must bring.
He resolves he will be like the trees

with their stolid silhouettes. He will stand,
the pink-streaked sky behind him,
anchored between day and dream.

How Should You Read the Moon?

Like an Arabic text, or how a dyslexic
meets the printed English word:
so when the slim crescent
begins to billow on the right
into a spinnaker of light,
you know the moon is fulling,
running with the wind.

As you climb the hill,
boulder of disease
upon your shoulders,
where should you look?
Down, with blinders on alone?
Better to look straight up
into the moon's old face.

Pause, breathe.
The moon is a rock
so strong it pulls waves
up a river against the natural current.

All night you needed to be brave,
but now the wind is falling.
Be still. Be filled.
Rest your head upon the pillow.

After the Tsunami

We stand on shoals of garbage,

look to the camera as if we'll find

our drowned love in the staring lens,

 or a message bearing an explanation

of how we slipped out of God's hands.

Bargaining

A white mist wraps around the dawn
as the river races downstream,
freed from ice at last,
seeking its mouth.

Only the crow speaks.
She caws, grieves for a mother
who bears the weight of her child
as she wades through a river,
the border between a here
and a there, twice a day,
seeking work.

The woman bribes guards
to keep from starving.

If the river could speak,
the river would ask
why?

Fear

We live on an island
surrounded by the sea
and we raise birds here.

We use the pure white
feathers of the eagle for our arrows.

We work hard to keep predators away,
but this morning I find
bloody feathers on the ground—
a song-bird, eyes glazed and empty,
body turning cold.

And now a sound— a plaintive mew—
a cat
leaps toward me,

a creature with hunting moons for eyes,
Cat
pushes its body against me,
serpent tail lashes at my legs. Horror

to feel the fur of a creature
I learned to fear
before I could talk
while I sat beside my elders,
inhaling rules, the entire island
a school

where I learned cats
will destroy with stalactite teeth
every ordinary sparrow.

Here on our island,
even when a bird dies
from the hand of a boy
who takes pleasure
in hurling stones,
we blame the cats.

Sing to the Boys

Stalled at the cusp of adolescence
when voice deepens, bones elongate,
the boys who were never sung to
leave the forest and appear at dusk.

The boys who were never sung to
fester inside a winter
they have conjured for themselves.
They pick their swaggering way

through patches of dirty snow.
It's always winter for the boys.
Sheltered coves have frozen,
and the boys

instead of fighting Hook,
have become Hook.
Shadow-capes flown back
they swarm one-handed over the sides

of schools, swashbuckling
fore to aft, steel hearts clanging
as they race down waxed linoleum floors
past hostile rows of lockers.

Half-blind, they see
only enemies stalking
the halls. No summer constellations
visible between football field and cloud.

Sing to the boys
that they might step into spring;
see clusters of white crocuses;
fall to their knees and love their lives.

A Call for 19th Century Painters

Cézanne, come back and paint
a landscape in oranges and greens,
a mountain top emerging on a hot,
dry afternoon, cicadas racketing,

the air still clear of diesel fumes,
and a call for you, Monet, to paint
a field of poppies unlinked to mercenary
middle men or sad girls coiled

on mattresses. And Gauguin,
amid the wreckage left by hurricanes,
we long for color and a sense of idyll
on an island, but you, Van Gogh, you

who stood staring up at stars and out at fields,
we need to heed how by using the flat side
of a knife to press sky and sunlight onto canvas,
you were trying to ride the wolf inside you.

How They Once Leapt

It was just a second ago,
a biological blink of the eye,
when the shoals of salmon
swam almost four thousand miles
through the cold Atlantic
from feeding grounds off Greenland
into Long Island Sound, and then surging upstream,
veered into the tributaries of New England's
rugged mountains, hurtling ever higher,

over falls,
endured droughts,
spawned under summer leaves,
held fast through winter,
and in the great cycle of the seasons,
were swept back in spring flooding
to the sea.

We've always read
the salmon's arduous journey
as hero on a quest—
the life force stripped of digression,
the concentration of desire,
and then we blocked the surge
with dams, provided lifts and ladders.

The city lights winked on,
and the light-struck streams went dark.

Creating Trails

We trim back feathery pine,
skirt the rim of the bog,
lop off dead limbs then climb
to the grove of beech trees,
poised elephant-legged
on the ridge. This is the path
we want you to follow.

From this point on
the way is clear.
You may traverse
the hill's slant, descend
knee-deep in cinnamon ferns,
pause at the pond's spongy edge.
Its peaty smell

may afflict you with longing
for summer (or your life)
never to end, but ducks
floating between lily pads
will calm you. You'll admire
the beavers' gnawed sculptures.
That's all we can do.

We can't predict
what tenderness
might be distilled
from the line of swamp maples
etched in the mist, what ache
might be soothed as a jay
scolds from the opposite shore.

The Verb To Be

So I had been trying to pysch myself into asking this really cute, nice guy
named Kyle to the prom
                but he sent Mindy a promposal via pizza, spelling out
Prom? in red-pepper letters. My friend Lisa said
                      *That's so cheesy, why do you
even like the guy?* Then Josh B., he's in my Spanish class, asked me
to go with him. Lisa said
                      *He's totally not cool, say no, and anyway
he just wants you
to do his homework,* but when he asked me
I felt this relief, like, whoa, I'm normal!!
                I mean half the time I feel like an irregular verb, like
I don't fit
the pattern.
So I said, *Si, yo voy contigo.* He didn't even smile. After that
it was so awkward being with him in class.
                    Like what did we have in common?
Do you have brothers or sisters? I asked him.
                    Two older brothers.
Pets?
                    Yeah. A German shepherd. His name is Max.
Why are you growing a moustache?
                  I have a baby face.
What did he ask *me*? Nothing. *Nada.* I couldn't help wishing
I was going with Kyle, but then I thought
                Kyle is a regular verb, easy
to memorize. Lisa said
                Prom dresses are so boring.
She's going to wear a tux. She's got way more guts than I do.
But then again she's been dating Anita for a year. One thing I've
noticed—
                love makes a person more secure. But the
virus
is here now, and prom's been called off. My dress was slinky,
shimmery and blue.
With little straps. I was going to be a mermaid.

Adjusting

The day after the doctor lops off
one velvet breast, she looks out the window,
sees a vine curled around a maple tree.

She lived neck-deep for fifty years
with the same man. He's gone now,
but she remembers their salty fights,

the bridges they built
to keep their pulsing intimacy.
I'm lop-sided, she cries, *I'm sorry,*

but he can't answer. She saw
his ghost sometimes when she rose
early for a swim. A hummingbird darts

to the cup of nectar just outside. Yellow jackets
swarm there, too. Jays make a racket in the pines.
Wings beat against her chest.

A New Country

Once upon a time I studied
the lines and contours of your face,
and a map took shape, a new country,
in which I saw paths ending

in astonishing views, a coastline
adorned with white beaches—
Rio before Portugal polluted her—
no litter, and King Ego did not rule

this country, only a council of three men,
three women, all of whom knew
the guidebook to our desires.
The currency was humor,

the language spoken, nuanced,
and every evening we visited
that secret place behind the waterfall,
your hand in mine, my love.

Bequest

May I leave you
pine needles,
a century's worth,
creating a springy duff

underfoot, the high-pitched
scree of young eagles,
and heron surprise
as mist disperses,

revealing the singular pewter
blue of the river in August,
and may I leave you
August's pink phlox

and the orange-black kings
and queens flirting
in milkweed,
followed by rusting ferns

and the certainty
that after the snow,
white stars
will dot the bracken.

This, I pray, goes to you.
Not plastic in ditches,
not graveyards for cars.

Monster

Each passing generation longs for
the Loch Ness monster
to surface. One does wonder
what Nessie has been doing
all this time under the white-tipped waves.

Does she circle the lagoon
in one direction only,
stretching her periscope neck
to learn secrets whispered
along the shore?

Why is the monster so shy?
What is she waiting for?

When death comes at last to Nessie—
(How many centuries has it been?)
will she rise to the top, belly up?
And when the autopsy is performed,
a crowd gathered on the beach, will we find
the strands of DNA that at last explain
monster? Will we finally understand
the mind behind the impulse
to drop chemicals on children?

On the Flight from Boston to San Francisco

The large man besides me yells
at the woman in front of him, pudgy
hand pressed in desperation against
the encroachment of her seat. A young child
cries. A curious tension fills the plane as everyone
ignores her. A woman traces our progress across her screen
while two seats to the right, humans dressed as rabbits
cavort beneath a tree. Outside my window jagged
mountain tops come into view, snow in places,
and tadpole-shaped incursions into forests. Clearings
for houses, or perhaps vestiges of an extinct civilization.

Ennui

You'd think by now we'd be bored
silly by death, after all, even before
the pandemic, 105 people died
each minute, 55.3 million people died
each year. Look at all the cemeteries,
the stupas, and listen to the elegies—how Mom
always burned the beans—how Dad was always
there for us, and hear the clop of riderless white
horses, see all the bodies found under rubble—
the latest drone strike, hurricane, or earthquake—
and let's not forget what happens when bacteria
inhabits lettuce, or the 2,000-plus types of cancer,
nor, of course, the virus that is laying waste
to countless lives. You'd think by now
death would be a sort of background noise,
the hum of traffic, but no, death still
startles us, takes us by surprise, turns us
upside down and inside out as if it had never
happened to anyone before.

The Hike

End of April in Northern California
along the coast. My niece leads us
through a sort of rain forest,
past goblin trees and trumpet-vines.

Large beads of moisture coalesce
in rows on leaves as if a giant
had been crying. Orange slugs on steroids
guard our way. The trail is ditched

and ankle-turning. My niece strides ahead
until my brother slips, falls, has trouble
getting to his feet. I hold out my hand
to help him. The seven years between us

keeps shrinking, though there was a time
he was a minor god. I'm more aware than ever
that in the not-too-distant future, there will be
no more of him, of me. Hikers with casual California

cheerfulness pass by, say hi. My brother offers chocolate,
the charm that cures all ills. We gather up our stuff,
climb on. As if it were the Chinese New Year,
yellow flowers with orange spikes dot the bank

like dancing dragons. Thick air disperses.
Light-filled as lanterns,
we rise to view the ocean.

Phantom Dog

Several times lately in the middle of the night
I am startled awake by a barking dog.
I reach out to find my own dog
lying stretched out, nose
near my toes, deep in sleep.

I think of Mary Oliver's one, wild,
precious life. How I ought be living it.
I think of Voltaire's garden.
How I ought to be cultivating it.
My dog twitches beside me,
my parents speak to me,
I see my husband's face.

It's already early dawn
filled with the first singing of birds.
The planet turns.
The phantom dog barks.

Plain Song

A pair of doves
roosting in the eaves
performs a duet
as I slip out of the house,
just me floating down
a small, cobblestoned alley
to buy a baguette, he still sleeping,
his boat-sized boots beside
my small ones on the tiled floor.
Yesterday we finally found
the ruined castle we'd spied
on a distant hill.

We are not getting along, both of us
charging down a New York City
sidewalk. The cherry trees
hold knots of sparrows,
gossiping as if they've known
each other forever. We slow down,
start over.

A week after his death,
it's just me again,
walking the woods' path.

A bird lands in a small pine
just to one side, a fat, round
chickadee, and then another, and another,
until ten birds ornament the tree
and sing in unison.

Their five notes,
a micrometer off in pitch,
collide. A slight buzz rises.

It's just like him
to arrange this. Just odd enough.
His sense of humor.

Cricket Song
(Zuihitsu)

Crescent moon, you bloom in the blue space where bats swirled earlier this summer.

We light the fire-pit and draw in close. My daughter-in-law is seven months pregnant.
I know the baby is a boy.

The moon is always a surprise, whether it's between tall buildings or pines at the edge of our woods.

The occasional cricket still chimes, even though the time for mating has come and gone.

The singular cadence of each person's voice braids into a rope, a lifeline.

In the morning, lady bugs sashay across the window, their little legs churning as they race across the glass. My legs must have looked like that when I was small, walking in the woods with my father.

The news then was not so terrible, as it is now, day after day.

A house filled with sleeping people feels different from an empty house.

The chairs around the firepit still seem to hold each one of us.

I imagine teaching my grandson how to toast marshmallows. If he burns his fingers I will distract him—

Listen, I'll say, One time when I was a child I flew straight up to the moon, opened a door, and stepped inside and met the old man who lives there with his dog.

It was then I learned that it's not crickets you're hearing in late October, but the old man singing.

My Invention

Today I am going to invent joy.
I will need one child,
a pair of small hands,
and a bowl of soap suds.

I'm going to win the Nobel Prize
in a category not yet
imagined by the Committee,
but rest assured these fine

personages will be dressed
to the nines, smart in tweed suits, trim
in black dresses. Their eyes will shine
with excitement as the chairperson

announces this extraordinary achievement
in the history of humankind
as we stand where portraits of past
winners line the walls in gold frames—

physicists, doctors, writers, chemists,
and let's not forget those who worked
to bring peace, yes, imagine, this—peace—
to the world, and the members of the Committee

will clap me on the back and say
in their elegant accents, What a gift
you have given the world. I shall bow,
say thank you, then lead the Committee

to the bank of a river, where we shall gather
in silence. The scent of mint will rise.
Eagles will play in the thermals.
There will be no speeches.

Flight

A downy, white feather snagged on a cattail
blows like a flag in the breeze
at the edge of the river bank
where in March I watched a pair of swans,
pen and cob, bending their necks,
pulling, placing, pulling, placing
one straw, another straw,
a reed, a cattail, day after day,
until they'd constructed a rafty nest.

I don't know how many times the heron
landed beside them, folding its neck
into a question mark before one by one,
grey and glistening, six new swans pecked
their way into this river world,

and now on a late-summer morning,
the female glides through mist,
her cygnets following. Brown feathers
now instead of grey, interspersed
with white. They are almost ready
to fly, and I think of my son,

how many years ago we sat in the diner,
the one near the dam and the fish-run,
where in 1909 the owner of the logging company
fell to his death when his fancy motor-car
slipped over the falls. Same place where in 1647
the Peskeompscuts were slaughtered
at dawn by an English captain,

and we were enjoying a farewell lunch
before his move to New York City,
when a mothering devil
provoked me into giving advice,

one last chance to save him
from every possible misstep,
so "Blah blah blah," I said,
and to my relief he simply nodded and smiled,
then looking around at all the kitsch,
at the giant spoon and fork on one wall
and the thirty clocks surrounding us, he said,
"It's sort of creepy; I wouldn't want to be here
by myself in the dark," and I told him,

when I was twelve my mother took me
to see the Ingmar Bergman film,
Wild Strawberries—the characters spoke Swedish,
but as we were living in Brazil, the subtitles
were in Portuguese, and I had no idea
why an old man wearing a suit was climbing
into a coffin, or why a grandfather clock
without hands loomed up behind him.
I had nightmares for weeks about coffins and clocks.

"I thought the film was going to be
about the sunlit days of childhood,
of coming upon clusters of sweet, red fruit," I said,
and he laughed, and I thought, This is the way it always is—
I'm either looking for my own childhood
or for his. He said he hadn't seen the movie
but would like to—and in that congenial moment,
the hands of the clocks lunged simultaneously
for the top of the hour, and it was time for him to go.

People can't seem to agree if this grace
of neck and white feathers, this creature
of myth and fairy tale, the mute swan,
Cygnus olor, is invasive or native,
destructive or helpful, but now
as the mother nudges one of her young,
I seem to hear her speak:

*Before your wings broaden,
into the potent span of a fully-grown cob,
I cannot imagine how you will manage to lift
the heft of your body into the air,
but I will be here to hear the great thrashing
as it reverberates along the shore.*

Radiant Geraniums

I require nothing more of you
than your extravagant redness,

but wonder are you pensive or restless
sitting in pots on my indoor porch?

Do you hear the creak of crows outside
as loneliness or desire for spring?

Perhaps you'd rather the romance
of a window-box, green shutters

against a white-washed house,
your petals drifting through air,

until they punctuate the cobblestones
below, where framed in the doorway,

a widow stands in black. Or do you long
for your roots to grow uncontained, scrawling

down and down forever through dirt?
I am a widow now myself.

As he did, I bend to dead-head
your crumpling blossoms,

snap your stems just at the joint
where they attach to the whole.

There are no answers.
Only your earthy, lemon-pepper,

alive
green scent.

The Fig Tree

1.
The fig tree's flower
blooms inside itself,
an interior garden,
a nursery for wasps,
where males and females
fulfill invisible and complicated
roles. One lays eggs;
one digs escape tunnels,
so life may go on.

I made dinner; you washed the dishes.
I day-dreamed; you watered the plants.

2.
The fig tree is shedding something sticky
all over the floor and on the little plants
that live beneath it. It's called scale,
the hard k sound landing like a curse
from the gods, and setting in motion
a memory: The Wednesday afternoons
my fingers didn't want to run from middle C
up to the next C, and it makes me reflect
on the magnitude and smallness of things, but size
can be hard to define: would you call a cancer cell
with its power to divide and swallow,
vanquish and diminish, large or small?

3.
The fig is a weeping fig,
the *benjamin ficus*, although
I'm not a botanist and prefer just plain fig
to ficus, finding fig a friendly word,
and pocket-sized. O Fig, I do wonder, if
we have we been wrong all these years
to take you from your native land? Doves
should be singing in your branches.

4.
I carry our tree outside—for it's *our* tree
now, you see—and spray it twice over
with a soapy mix, then rinse, and yet,
along the midrib of each leaf,
reddish specks line up like trucks
outside a diner. Q-tip in hand,
I wipe the little buggers away,

and then because it's supposed to rain
I leave our fig outside, thinking the natural
world will do it good, but all night,
while I'm safe inside, warm by a fire,
it storms—how could I have left
an indoor plant so defenseless
against the elements, like the men
I see in cardboard nests or the women
wrapped in plastic bags who toil uphill,
talking to themselves. The scale of fortune
tips toward the fortunate.

I should rise up, brave
the storm. But I can't move.
Why can't I rescue what I know
must be rescued? Morning dawns
sodden, subdued, a bit withdrawn,
but our fig tree still stands, lifts its leaves
in the morning breeze.

5.
Your leaves feel soft and smooth.
They are as figorously glossy
as they ever were, dark
against the clear pane of window.

O dear Fig,
can you please just stay alive?

Amy Gordon spent her childhood years in New England, France, England, and Brazil. Following a career of teaching theater skills to middle school students, she went back to school for an MFA in Poetry at Drew University. Her poems have appeared in *Blue Nib*, *The Massachusetts Review*, and other journals. Her first chapbook, *Deep Fahrenheit*, was brought out by Prolific Press in 2019. She is also the author of numerous books for young readers. *Painting the Rainbow* (Holiday House) won the 2015 Paterson Prize for Young People. She lives in Western Massachusetts.

www.ingramcontent.com/pod-product-compliance
Lightning Source LLC
LaVergne TN
LVHW041509070426
835507LV00012B/1447